An Ode to the Night

AF520397

An Ode to the Night

Kartikeya Atreya

DIGITALSPINES

First Edition, 2023

Copyright © Kartikeya Atreya, 2023

All rights reserved. No part of this publication may be reproduced, distributed, or transmitted in any form or by any means, including photocopying, recording, or other electronic or mechanical methods, without the prior written permission of the author, except in the case of brief quotations embodied in critical reviews and certain other non-commercial uses permitted by copyright law. For permission requests, write to the publisher.

This book can be exported from India only by the publishers or by the authorized suppliers. Infringement of this condition of sale will lead to Civil and Criminal prosecution.

Paperback ISBN: 978-81-979302-9-4
eBook ISBN: 978-81-979302-7-0
WebPDF ISBN: 978-93-95986-73-1

Note: Due care and diligence has been taken while editing and printing the book; neither the author nor the publishers of the book hold any responsibility for any mistake that may have inadvertently crept in.

The publishers shall not be liable for any direct, consequential, or incidental damages arising out of the use of the book. In case of binding mistakes, misprints, missing pages, etc., the publishers' entire liability, and your exclusive remedy, is replacement of the book within one month of purchase by similar edition/reprint of the book.

Published by DIGITAL SPINES.
Originally published by 16Leaves.

Printed and bound in India.

To whomever it may concern,
Don't panic.

Acknowledgement

I would like to start this book by first expressing my gratitude and appreciation for those around me. My family, immediate and extended, my friends and my peers and the teachers I have had over the years. They have all had a major part to play in the making of this book. But since the first time someone asked me who I would like to thank, three names have stuck out.

Before any of them, however, I have to thank my parents. They have raised me and are the sole reason I am the way I am. While the days have been far from perfect, I am nothing if not in eternal debt to both of them and of course, my brother. They have undoubtedly had the largest impact out of the whole world, perhaps not on this book, but in making me, 'me'.

Apart from them, the first of the people I would like to thank is Shayne Rajesh. Somebody I have known for half my life. Honestly, words fail me when I try describing the bond I have with Shayne. From the height of intelligence to the depths of stupidity, if there's one soul on this planet who wouldn't question anything before jumping in with me, it's Shayne. Regardless, he is one of the kindest people I've ever met and it's an honor to call him my friend.

Next is Shaurya Singh, someone who literally flipped my life around when I met him. While I haven't known him for the longest time, it amazes me, the effect he has had on my life. And I'm really not sure how I'll ever let him know how thankful I am. He manages to be smart and profoundly dull at the same time, and I honestly admire him for it. I wouldn't like our friendship to be any other way.

And last but not least, we have Srinath S. P. I would like to not thank Srinath for playing any sort of role related to this book or its creation. I would like to thank him for the near hundreds of hours we have spent together on the most pointless things. I would like to thank him for picking me, out of this whole world, to stick with. For all the things we have done together and all the things we haven't, I want to thank Srinath from the bottom of my heart for being Srinath. He means more to me than I could have ever imagined, and I wouldn't be who I am today without him.

And for everyone who has been there for the journey, thank you.

That's all for tonight folks.

Godspeed and goodwill.

Foreword

Kartikeya has always been slightly different. Even as a child I remember hearing him talk to himself or make up new stories through lyrics he had heard in a song. He has always been a fan of storytelling. While this book does not particularly exemplify that, I do believe it represents his second love—literature.

In this journey of 16 years I watched him grow and shape up into a confident teenager. So much so that today he has written a book. Though *An Ode to the Night* is his first book getting published, I have seen him write on varied topics since the age of eleven. He had impeccable concentration and started reading and writing very early, always selecting themes with maturity and complexity above his age.

As his mother, I always loved seeing him evolve and take this hobby of writing into something serious. *An Ode to the Night*, is a collection of poems written on a variety of themes, emotions and beliefs. It's his own labor of love which has my blessing. May this just be the beginning of his journey as a writer. And as always, I would like him to know that he has my constant support and love.

I hope you enjoy reading this book as much as I enjoyed watching him write it.

Pallavi Atreya

MA B.ed

Bangalore

Contents

I

Sorrow

1 Grief

It is, I believe, the most difficult thing to perceive.
An expression of sadness.
Grief so great, one can't help but let it out.
Poems and songs of heartbreak,
Murals of guilt and ever consuming remorse,
Songs of dreams only glimpsed. Realized, but for a mere moment.
Are we not fragile then?
To be so weak, to need to spread the sadness that burdens us so,
Or are we not strong?
To carry great scars and greater memories,
Yet still to move on,
Our hearts pumping with blistering might,
Ready once again to fight the battles it has lost.
So, as I watch, you let out your sigh of exhaustion
Your eyes watching the stars,
Wishing you were among them.
The moonlight lightens your tired face.
The distance between us, tiny. So why do I feel so far away?
Alas, the world is unfair.
And perhaps we are destined to suffer so near one another, but never to meet.

2 Remembrance

I've gotten over you
Memories of your flesh on mine like specks of star dust at the tip of my fingers.
The places you would kiss and hold me.
Have you found your replacement yet?
A new canvas to paint on?
A new piece of clay to mold to your liking?
Is that all I was?
Or were the moments we shared real?
So here I'll wait, in Purgatory
Because what we had is dead now,
A permanent eclipse of emotions.
I can't tell if I miss or despise you.
How have I moved on when I still think about you?
How can I move on when the marks of love you left on my flesh still persist?
How can I move on when your memory is still a fresh imprint on my lips?

How can I so easily learn to hate,
The one that taught me to love?

And still I try to decide on sleepless nights,

Were the moments we had real?

3 Tragedies

The greatest tragedies are about those left behind.
The saddest tales are of the aftermath.
The most painful burden to carry is to keep going on.
To move and shift focus.
The burn of unanswered questions and empty conversations.
To move on even if there is no end.
And such is human life,
Of those on this mortal plane.
A condition of no future,
A path of eternal destruction and rebuilding.
A condition of wretched survival.
To see no light,
No relief and no rest
But to continue on this tireless path.
To crawl through hell and back, even if there is nothing to crawl back to.

4 Lapse

I'd talk for days at a time.
Spinning webs of fables.
All connected,
Beginning to end.
And each sentence would be perfectly crafted.
I would give speeches and sermons.
And as I'd look up,
I'd find myself alone.
Talking to an echoing void.
My voice carried in that ceaseless night to no end;
To fall on no ears.
Rock walls and thunderstorms,
Crushing waves and screaming wind.
It all still feels so empty.
Like a permanent cowl
Shrouding my vision.
This world is pale and uninteresting.
Vapid and boring.
And everyone is stuck here together.
And compassion is an act long forgotten,
These blank faces would not know a confession if it was looking them in the eyes.
They simply can't find it in them

To care.
And I am no different,
Becoming an empty cog
In this machine I loathe.
And we're all sinners here
Empty and depraved.
It's not always their fault,
Not everyone is themselves the reason they are broken.
But even Hell is full of men who only ever made
One mistake.

5 End of the road

It was as if the world had failed.
It was gone in a moment,
But it took with it all joy.
Only dread and despair were real for a mere moment.
Tried and tested,
No journey is adequate.
No training is ample.
And a great air of crushing defeat covered the oceans themselves.
And it was a tear that fell,
On the floor.
How powerful,
Must tears be.
To be as the ocean.
It was as if the earth held such great sadness,
It passed it onto man.
And
It can do nothing but watch helplessly.
As its children walk with its own flaws.
How tragic,
For a mother to watch her children bear scars of battles they never fought.
But as a mother does,
She must fight on.
She must persist and hope,

She teaches better than her own mother did.
So her children
May not pass on more scars.
It was a tear that fell,
It was the eyes it fell from that hurt me so.
Was it even supposed to?
Was it meant to?
Was it worth it,
Being this sensitive?
I do not wish to carry these scars anymore.
They do not fit my skin.

6 I'm forgetting

Those fragmented lips,
They're gone now, almost.
I do not remember your smell,
The way you'd turn around when I called your name.
Our time together slipped through my fingers
like sand,
And now I find myself buried in it.
Locked out of the world in my own coffin of dust.
I do not remember how we'd dance together,
Counting the stars that rest above us,
Nestled into nebulas so very far away from us.
I do not remember what your laugh sounds like
anymore.
Is this really what I wished for?
To forget this part of my life?
To forget you and all we did together?
It is a curse to remember,
A sin to forget.
And I lack the strength to tell you.
I'm afraid that this too, will fall on uninterested ears.
That it, like so many questions before it, will be laid
to rest, never to be remembered.
Was I one of those questions for you?
To be heard and forgotten?
To never be paid a second thought,

A modicum of attention?
Perhaps I was.
But your silence,
The one you answered me with,
Filled this lonely abyss I called my life.
It was my fault.
It was I, after all, who mistook silence for approval.

7 Falter and fall

Twisted and bent is my view of this world
I see monsters.
Each face is a fragment,
To be studied and discarded.
That is, the price.
I further lose touch with this reality
I look in mirrors,
Not in vain,
But to remind myself
That I exist.
That this corrupt psyche
Has indeed, physical form.
My broken lens,
Clouded by hatred and anger,
Now blinds me.
At first I saw this world through rage.
Now I see nothing but scorn.
Flaws.
Reflections of my past.
Consequences of my mistakes.
I wish to see again.
To see how beautiful the sky is.
How beautiful life is.
Humanity and the perpetual struggle.
The beauty of our minds and skin.

Of scars and stories.
Of this world.
Instead,
I feel nothing but disgust.
I see brands, not scars.
Permanent reminders of those I did wrong.
I see mistakes and imperfections.
I see what I have done.
What have I become.
I do not feel anymore.
It's numbing.
And to not feel, is to not be human.
To be born is to be a man.
But to have a soul, is to be human.
I gaze in mirrors and do not recognize what
stares back.
I gaze inwards and see nothing.
I have become the unwanting emissary of anger.
Stuck in a twilight of realities.
Stuck between the path I have chosen and the past
I have woven.
I wish to be far away.
This house reeks of my failures.
This body burns with my sins.
They say you die twice in this world,
But who will remember the man who died each
moment he was alive?

8 Like tears in rain

So once again,
I sit in solitude.
Closed are the gates to this godforsaken town.
Buried in dust and the ash of my past.
No longer will the venom flow.
Decay, burn and rave in my iron tomb.
So once again,
I sit on this decrepit throne of thorns.
Once again, its iron teeth dig into my flesh.
This seat of malice and rage.
Only born to consume.
I despise what has happened.
I grow tired of what is happening and frightful of
what is to happen.
Yet once again,
I will crown myself.
I know that I must.
Neither a good choice, nor a noble one.
It is but the path I must walk again.
As I swore.
Blister and burn
On this path of burning corpses.
Smoldering fires and floating ash.
So once again,
I sit in my fallen kingdom.

My castle of iron and rot,
Seeps into me.
The iron teeth grind and twist.
They contort and crush.
But I swore.
So once again,
The rot consumes.
The teeth bite.
Closed are these ungodly gates in the land of ghosts.
In the kingdom of perpetual rain.
Where the madman who calls himself a fool lives.
All you will hear are cries and laughter,
All in agony.
The rain can wash away your tears,
But can it wash away the eyes that bleed them?

II

Rebirth

9 A ballad for mere men

What must a man do?
When his world comes crumbling down?
When his ideas collapse under their own weight?
When his perception is cracked and broken,
His mind is tired, his eyes grow weary of the woe he witnesses.
His bones lack the strength to go on and he wishes for the warm embrace of his mother.
But this world knows no such comfort. No soothing words may he hear this snowy night.
No arms may wrap themselves around him and no familiar voice may tell him,
"It is all right. You have fought long enough. Now you may rest."
No!
This world knows naught, the journey this man has taken!
And no!
This world knows naught, the pains this man has suffered!
And so his tears fall on the empty floor of the manor he built, on the desolate path he took.
For it was anger that was taught to him.

It was hatred that was instilled in him.
It was pain.
It was pain that was carved into him.
In streaks and brands across his flesh,
He carries this pain. This pain that molded him.
And now it is the same world that asks his to shed himself of this curse.
To leave behind what has become a part of him.
To be better.
But how can a man be better,
Be better than the world that surrounds him?
Be better than all he has ever seen?

How can he be better if he was never taught to love himself?
If he was never taught to be kind to himself?
How can a man love, if he does not know how to?
If he is too afraid to truly care for someone more than himself?
If he was never taught that this world does not have to be faced alone?
If he was never taught that there are those in this world that care,
That love and kindness exist still,
That this cold world knows too, warmth and comfort, beauty and peace.
That there are, in fact, eyes that wish to be locked with his.
Lips that wish to meet his, arms that wish to hold his

And a voice that wishes to serenade him, take him far away,
A land of dreams, where compassion knows no bounds, where his head is held up high,
Where the callouses on his hands do not burn, and where his shoulders are not burdened
By the world.
Where his tears do not stream down his face in agonizing silence,
Where his sadness, too, has found a voice.
And his past, too, has come forth, to give way to his future.
Where strength has given way to courage, where anger has given way to patience, where hatred has given way to humility.
Where he can speak as he feels
Where he can, once again feel the warmth of the Sun on his skin.
Where he is not afraid of himself. Where he is not afraid of the path that lies ahead of him.
Where he knows, if he ever wishes to return, he will find himself welcome with open arms.
And he opens his eyes. And sees specks of stardust far above him.
He sees flowing rivers of radiant light,
He sees cosmic vistas beyond all he is,
A veil of stars blanketing it all,
Covered with astral dew.

And in that moment, he understands,
"How can one man be expected to conquer this universe alone?"
Nay, he is not.
No man may, nor can he go above the mortal plane which he himself inhabits.
No man may crown himself ruler of these vast fields of Elysium.
And fear not! It is not because of fear of a higher power,
It is not due to fear of judgment,
Nor holy salvation, nor Earthly rebirth.
It is because he does not need to.
He does not need to sacrifice all he has, simply to realize a truth few understand truly.
There is no purpose in this great struggle of ours.
There is no rhyme or reason in this battle known as the human condition.
And one day, he will awaken and arise to this realization.
And he will still choose to struggle. He will still choose to fight.
He will choose to go against the meaningless of it all.
He will choose to give his fleeting life meaning, in this ocean of absurdity.
He will realize, his body is not meant to hold such rage within it.

So, even in this barren, meaningless existence, he
will love.
He will make purpose.
He will become more than he ever was.
He will grow.
And he will rise,
From the ashes of his past self,
Higher than he has ever been,
In this infinite universe,
Only when he becomes nothing,
Will he become everything.
He will truly be, infinite.

Bound by no testaments,
Nor of man or God.
Held down by no regrets,
No past.
He sees only himself as he is now.
For the past is a river that has already gone by,
And the future is a waterfall one cannot see past.
And it is in this uncertainty,
He smiles, as he feels the warmth of the Sun on
his skin.
For he is afraid no more.
He knows, no matter what happens,
The Sun shall still rise,
And the birds shall still sing,
The World shall still move on,

So why must he stop?
And he knows he will not.
He has faith in his strength, and in himself.
He knows, what can be broken down, can be rebuilt stronger than before.
And such is the path of man, for he himself is the marble, and the sculptor.
In such uncertainty, is where lies true strength.
In such acceptance, is where lies peace.
In such fear, is where lies courage.
And only when a man's tears fall to the ground, can a garden of his labors begin to grow.
Only when he accepts the world for what it is, will he find peace in it.
Only when he accepts what he is, will he find the ability to become better.
It is all right. You have fought long enough. You did well. Now you may rest.

10 Defeat

And it is in that moment,
In untold agony,
Facing his greatest challenge,
He knows not, whether it is the rain, or his tears which stream down his face
The distant boom of lightning thunders across the valley, but he hears it not.
He looks up, only to realize a moment too late,
There is nobody to answer his prayers any longer.
He can slowly feel it now,
A creeping realization he ignored until then.
Like a fissure slithering across the length of his body,
The fatigue and pain take their hold.
His body and mind alike,
Trained to not perceive limits, to go through any obstacles in their way,
Honed to perfection, have crossed their final limit.
For just because it cannot be seen, does not mean it is not real.
Just as the grip of the lady in black,
Which already clutches the warriors weeping heart in her cold grasp.
And he falls to his knees, stripped of honor and battle scars.

Vulnerable once again, as a newborn child, he is
unveiled.
No more armor covers his mortal shell,
No further lies hide his soul.
And it is in that moment, as he lies in the rain,
defeated, broken and dying.
He holds out his hand, perhaps to grasp a face not
really there,
It is met with that of his comrade.
It is in that moment, he calls out, and there is only
one word he has the strength to utter.
"Ma"

11 Fatherhood

They took away my father.
I don't know where he went,
I don't know why he left.
But one day I woke up and he was gone.
In his place was another, different man.
This one smiles less often.
He isn't always happy,
He isn't always free for me.
He's busy and stressed.
He has flaws.
But he laughs the same as my father did
He hugs me the same as my father did.
He leaves me wondering,
Where did my father go?
And now I know.
He took those things and gave them to me.
He left me wondering,
Do I hate myself or the parts of me my father
  gave me?

How do I be better than the world if it's the only
  world I've ever seen?
I do not feel jubilant as I once did,
This world has made me uncomfortably aware of all
  the sorrows that plague it.

Fewer reasons to smile, to dance, to simply be happy.
I just keep myself busy to not worry about it.
An idle mind is the devil's workshop, I remember.
So I keep my head down, and I work.
I wonder,
Was the world always this bleak and flawed?

12 Sacrifice

How long will you stay down?
Beaten and broken?
How long will you wallow and cry?
Burdened by this world's cruelty,
Bruised by its uncaring nature?
When will you realize that it is only you
Who changes, not this world.
"Tomorrow. I'll do it tomorrow"
Tomorrow arrives, but it changes nothing.
Tomorrow is more excuses.
Tomorrow is failure.
If the world's eternal blizzard is what has broken you so,
When will you realize,
You yourself have to be the bonfire your soul needs.
This world is hollow.
Long and alone is the path you must trek.
So when will you realize,
Nothing in this world can give you the relief you want so dearly,
Except you.
This world will not relent, it will not give you a moment of peace, until you create it.
Until you build it.

Happiness is a work of art,
Blood sweat and tears are the paint.
Happiness isn't found, stumbled upon,
Given.
Happiness is work. Struggle.
Happiness is sacrifice.
So what are you willing to sacrifice
For yourself?

13 Among the stars

Oh we all have a place among the stars.
I remember
The old man sitting next to the train tracks used to tell me.
He'd sit and patiently wait each day
And I'd sit with him and we'd think out loud together.
He'd tell me great stories,
Fables of lands far away.
Tales spun in warm nostalgia,
He'd remember wrong sometimes and correct himself.
He would never be wrong about the trains, though. He knew those better than he knew himself.
He'd mention how much time he spent studying them.
And each day he'd tell me
Oh we all have a place among the stars.
And I'd question that,
But he was adamant.
His eyes in dreams dreamt long ago,
His calloused hands in tired retreat.
If there was a destination to this life,
He must have reached it long ago.
So I asked him
Among which stars do you dwell?

And he was silent.
And with his voice went the whistling of the wind,
The rustling of the leaves.
And he didn't answer.
For days I'd return to those tracks and we'd share
  silence together.
And that is when my mother told me,
Not to talk to the drunkard by the train tracks,
For he lost his mind long ago, along with his wife.
So the next time I saw him,
My question was different
What was she like, the love of your life?
And he answered not.
Days passed and only one of my desires was fulfilled.
He spoke, slowly and steadily,
As if reciting something he practiced long ago.
There are some, boy. Who do not belong among the
  stars. May their place be taken by one more worthy.
Oh, we all have a place among the stars,
But even in a universe of light,
There will be those that dwell in the darkness.
And it seemed that day,
The world wept as he did.
And before I knew it,
It would be the last time I would see those aged eyes,
Though they looked young today.
And it was the last time I would see those
  tired hands,
Though today they were free of burden.

And his bent back was free of guilt.
And even though the sky wept, as it had for days,
He spoke clearly and happily.
As if he was speaking from the heart.
And it was only then he told me,
After months of sitting next to those train tracks,
It was only then he told me
How his wife used to sit next to him,
By the train tracks.
And they'd wonder out loud together.
She'd tell him stories and he'd tell her how much he hated trains.
And so it was tragic,
The railway accident that took her away from him.
And that was the last time I saw the old man by the train tracks,
A permanent reminder to himself about all that he had lost.
He had become a walking mausoleum.
And so he remembered her the only way he could.
And as I went back to the tracks the next day,
I was satisfied, in perhaps misguided joy,
That I had shown him some happiness before he went.
Before he went,
To his place among the stars.

14 One final step

But it is.
It always has been.
Such is the nature of life.
Such is the nature of man.
To hope for a better future.
To build one.
To fight for one.
This world is cruel and alone,
And that is why it is you who must be better.
Be kind.
Be compassionate.
For what else is life?
An empty journey with no end?
Of course not.
It is the journey which is life.
And its purpose is to struggle.
For, you see, this path you have taken,
Is yours to take.
It is yours to shift and mold.
It is human nature,
To rise above that meaningless.
To be better than the world that surrounds us.
So make a better world,
For yourself and for those around you.
Find joy in knowing,

You made a difference.
A difference worth making.
I wish you calm skies and a kinder sea, oh traveler.
May you see the most majestic sights this world has
to offer.
May you spread more joy and love than you received.
May you find strength and peace,
To be better than those that came before you.
May you find the ability,
To make a better world,
For some other than yourself.

15 Light

Let us see,
Oh traitor.
Who stands tall,
When judgment reins free.
I know I have sinned.
I know I have made mistakes.
But I choose to be better.
I choose to rise above my past.
I choose not to be blind to this world,
For I see it as you do.
I simply choose to make it better
For those that shall walk it after me and you.
So let us see,
My brother in arms.
May our story be told ages after it has ended.
May our souls live on without these mortal shells to bind them;
May our fate, wound and entrenched in pain,
Be etched into the lush ground beneath my feet.
And while I do not wish for my land to bear the scars of battles I have fought,
Let it be so for this once.
Let it be a lesson and a warning.
Let your defeat teach you as well,
The value in kindness.

And it shall be my weakness that tells these stories.
The tempered souls and capable hands I trust in.
And let your defeat teach you as well,
My brother.
The value of faith, and of true strength.
And may you see radiant light,
When it is my kindness that spares your
  wretched soul,
And reveals to you,
Reality.

16 The head

It's a mirror.
That voice inside of you,
Clawing at your mind.
Festering in the dark.
This world only has one constant.
Experience.
How one reacts the experience is what changes.
Two sides of the same coin.
How much has your past shaped you?
Molded you?
Have you sought to avoid it?
Fight it?
Never repeat it?
Have you realized,
That it does not make you what you are?
That you are more than the scars you bear?
That you can go beyond what you have experienced.
Do you see,
What your hands can create,
Once you free them of the shackles of your past?
Do you see,
The strength that lies in your mind,
Once you rid yourself from your past's shadow?
Once you stop lurking in the dark,
Once you stop limiting yourself,

Once you feel the warmth of the Sun once again
And the Moon's lovely touch on your skin once again.
Once you struggle and fight,
To rise above yourself.
Do you see,
How infinite you are?

17 Rain

Be water my friend.
Formless,
Boundless,
Limitless.
Understand, once you lose shape,
You lose the limitations that come with it.
Be gentle as rain,
Calming to the soul,
Nourisher of the world.
Be steadfast as a stream,
To find a path in the most unlikely of places,
To never stop moving.
Be valiant as a river,
Providing haven to all those in need,
Sweet with the gift of life.
Be unmoving as the ocean,
Stand with no evil,
Know yourself and your own,
And leave not their side.
Leave not what is important to you.
Stand your ground, no matter the foe.
Lastly,
Be fearful as a riptide.
Be destructive as a cyclone.
To have the strength to stand up for yourself.

The courage to believe in yourself.
It is not destructive power you should strive for,
But ability.
To provide,
To protect,
To preserve.
You need not understand this world to be happy,
You must only understand yourself.

18 Burn and rave

So cower not, my dear.
This world is cruel and vast.
But so are you.
So vast and unfathomably beautiful.
Do not go gentle into that good night.
As the world sleeps,
Rise and burn.
Light up the night sky
Burn and struggle
In your glorious imperfections.
Struggle, because what is more human?
What is more human than to struggle,
Than to smile through blood
To grit your teeth and struggle?
Oh, if only you knew
How liberating it is to fight.
Fight, knowing you lived a good life.
Fight and fret not, for when you fall, I will be here.
Learn from my scars and pick the path not
  walked oft.
Repeat not, my mistakes and choices.
Be the beacon this world needs.
I too, will struggle, but my battle is different.
I am sorry I cannot be what I need to be.
But never will I let you walk this path.

This cloak of misery,
May it provide you warmth.
This cowl of hatred,
May it grant you safety.
This life of tragedy,
May it grant you lessons.
So fight.
Burn.
Struggle and
Rave.

19 Metamorphosis

For what is a man,
Who has lied?
Who has deceived?
Who has never truly lived the truth?
Never has he felt the wind of the righteous,
For he has engulfed himself,
In this cocoon of charades.
And in the frigid depth of solace,
It is the ivory hand of love,
Who reaches out in an attempt to set right what has gone awry,
To do right by those he calls his own,
To understand,
It is not a coffin in which he rests so,
But a cocoon.
Of obsidian silk and crimson hue,
The fetid stench of treachery enveloping it,
But a cocoon still.
So he must choose,
Whether to lie still,
Or to climb.
To rid this fabric of sin from his flesh.

To be reborn,
Become anew,
In new body and new mind,
To emerge as, perhaps,
A butterfly of new creation.

20 The Wall

When will you see,
It has always been in front of you.
The answer lies not behind twisting myriad paths,
But before you.
When will you understand, the responsibility
  bestowed upon you?
When will you learn to see things for what they are?
This world does not dance to your tune,
Charmer.
These shifting lands do not follow your footsteps,
Traveler.
I'm afraid it was the fall that blinded you,
When you first fell from those flowing fields,
Those ethereal pastures of beauty beyond mine
  and yours;
When you were cast down and couldn't help but look
  skywards,
Perhaps for an answer.
An answer you will never receive.
But in stubborn misery,
You journey still to the peak of that mountain.
You journey to find the light you once felt on your
  ashen skin.
The same light that drew clouds over your eyes.
This blindness that you mistake for ignorance,

Let it be your saving grace.
Let it shield you from the woes you must face
  one day.
Like another long before you,
Perhaps you, too, are cursed to carry this burden
  until the end of days.
Yet again I ask you,
Is it really a curse?
I watch, from a place far beyond your reach.
Each boulder,
Each drop of sweat and rain,
Each step,
Each doubt,
They must fortify you.
Temper your will until iron trembles before it.
You must be insurmountable.
Because as I see it, old friend,
It is only light that emanates from you.
It is only strength you radiate.
So,
As I see it, old friend,
I imagine you happy.

21 A ballad for the jester

That mask you dance with,
Only hides your beauty.
This performance of yours,
Will not help your solitude.
I hope you understand,
My friend,
It matters not, what mask you wear.
It matters not, what those eyes of emerald see.
It matters not, what tune you follow today.
It is only you that matters.
Disregard these ministers,
Them and their antics.
See that you belong among greater men.
Among mightier men.
See not only the path ahead of you,
But the treachery through which you have prevailed,
nay, conquered.
I hope you see, my friend,
That you are where you belong,
If you make it so.
If it is your truth you live,
If it is you yourself that you dance for,
I swear to you,

You belong.
In your glory and accolades,
Deservingly yours,
Achieved through trials of fire,
I have seen you conquer continents,
In a land where most fear adversity.
So even if without me,
Even in dark nights, where your company seems to be the lonely stars above,
Even as your eyes glisten and your shoulders fall,
I have seen few as capable as you.
I swear to you,
You belong.

22 Morningstar

Like a God you descended,
Something I could not even perceive.
Like a blessing,
You fell from the sky above.
I blame myself still,
Wondering if I'm worthy enough of this crown,
But it is your voice that serenades me repeatedly.
Do they still make your kind?
I feared they had been lost forever
To the dark recesses of this desolate kingdom.
It brings me great comfort that there are men such as you,
Who sing as you do,
In flowing silver sails.
Who walk as you do,
With autumn's spring in your step.
Perhaps there is a greater will indeed.
To grant this poor sinner a helping hand as yours.
I wonder if this debt will come due one day,
As do all of them.
But there's something in your eyes that makes me doubt this truth.
Sapphire gems of emerald hue,
The world pales in comparison to them.

While I do not deem myself worthy
Of this ichor your hands bleed,
Let me try.
And perhaps one day, I hope
My eyes shine like yours.

23 Destined to knot, not meet

How is it that you and I are so different?
You have seen the same vistas as I, if not more.
You have been there every step of the journey, longer than even I.
The stories I carry, so do you.
So how is it,
That our conflict is ever present?
Any attempt at peace fails,
Surrender works naught,
And neither does battle.
Are we meant to dance to this rhythm forever?
No matter how far away I get,
I gravitate back to this battle.
So how is it,
That through all these bitter years,
You have changed,
So have I,
But we have not.
It matters not the strides you or I make in our life,
Back here is where we'll find ourselves.
Some part of me finds comfort in it now.
Knowing no matter what,
Some things do not change.

So why is it,
Through thick and thin,
We still smile together?
We laugh like nowhere else?
This twisted comedy of errors,
Is this how it is meant to be?
Ah,
It matters not.
Come,
Let us argue again.
How else am I supposed to show you that I care?

24 To live without regrets

How can you be alive
Unless you have died?
How can you appreciate the Sun
Until you have faced the eternal night?
How can you walk this earth with joy
Until you have felt the blistering hatred seethe into your soul?
Down in the land
Where the dead are still walking
Where torment is the only reality you face
And the screams of the damned drown out your own.
How can you appreciate rolling hills and meadows of flowers
Until you have bathed in the fetid rapids of the Styx itself?
Until your back is torn and broken
Where these umbral walls have carved into them
Symbols of agony and anguish
Where the dome of the cosmos is fractured and broken?
How can you feel alive
Until you have locked eyes with Nyx herself,

Shaken hands with death,
And conquered the void;
Not of the eternal slumber, but the one that resides inside you?
The amalgamation of doubts, fears and questions you aren't brave enough to ask yourself
The shadow cast by your mind
Festers in rotting silence
And echoes across your very bones.
It feeds upon you,
Ever looming and threatening to drag you down into the depths of depravity.
It is once you conquer the void within yourself,
It is then you will realize that you are alive.
For a man who fears not himself,
Has nothing to fear in this world at all.

25 The son

Are you still watching?
Are you still behind me, to catch me if I fall?
Is it your hand I feel on my back
Or is that the rushing of the wind?
Am I still moving or has the world simply left me behind?
Is it darkness that surrounds me?
Or is there hope still?
If I was to turn back,
Would I find myself
Facing your memories?
Would it be your muted voice,
Buried under nostalgia?
Or would I find you standing tall in pride,
Your eyes, like summer's Sun.
Your face, like spring's bloom.
Am I taking the right steps?
Or have I strayed from my path?
Am I strong enough yet,
To carry this legacy passed on to me?
To carry the dreams of those that came before me?
And if I'm not,
Am I strong enough to carry yours?
Am I strong enough to walk on by myself?
Is it time now,

For my hand to be on your back?
I can only hope,
I can be half the man you are.
I can only hope,
It is your name that lives on through me.
I can only hope,
That you'll still be watching,
Even if you're oceans away from me.

26 The father

If I could, I would walk alongside you.
Never would you have to brave this world
With doubts in your mind.
Never would you face a challenge,
Wondering if failure would lead to solitude.
But it is not so,
And as much as I try,
I find myself guiding you to my path.
Dreams of mine that I was never brave enough to accomplish.
I hear my voice echoing with notes of anger,
Even if I do not want it to.
I suppose,
This twisted machinery we walk has locked me behind you,
To follow, and not journey with.
Perhaps it began a long time ago,
This tradition we join.
And now, this old man can only hope,
That you have the clarity to break it.
I can only hope,
That you can find it in your heart to forgive me.
For all I have done and for all I have not,
I can only hope you find peace.
Just know,

You needn't be strong enough to carry the dreams of
those before you, not even mine.
You must simply be strong enough to carry your own.
To carve your own path.
To not trek the route I myself followed.
And what more can this poor soul hope for?
Than for you to know.
While I could not be with you,
I was behind you, every moment.
And even now,
As these shifting tides warn me,
Times are changing once again.
What more can this poor soul hope for,
Than for you to know,
Even if I am far, far away,
In myriad lands beyond my mind,
I will always be right there with you.

III

Stardust and Sunshine

27 Morning Sun

All alone up in your lonesome domain.
Do you not feel alone,
Watching your children build great spires to perhaps
  one day reach you,
Knowing in your heart they never will?
To hold up this vast nebula,
Do you never wish to see what could have been?
In your phases and shifts,
Perpetual is our path together.
Perhaps it was written long ago,
Carved in some long forgotten obelisk
I would bear the weight of my existence,
And you would bear the weight of the worlds.
Long and desolate is the path to you.
Yet, we suffer together.
Yet, we stay together.
In that intimate orbit of ours.
Through time and tide.
Maybe I can learn from you
And you, from me.

28 It's a small world, in none of the right ways

It's a cruel world we live in.
Not because of some human flaw or the sheer size of it.
But because, if there's anything my time on it has taught me,
It's that nothing really makes sense.
There are flaws to be seen in everything.
Ideologies, schools of thought,
Even coping mechanisms.
There really isn't a concrete way of living, is there?
You think you have things figured out, and then before you know it,
The days bleed into each other,
Getting out of bed is difficult
And your body doesn't seem to move as it used to.
There are bits of you in every person I see.
It's like my mind can't let go of your face.
I remember it so well,
I constantly see it.
And it's that cycle,

That repetitive feeling of ending up back at
square one.
You'd really think someone would have figured it out
by now.
Well if there's anything you wish to learn from me,
You're a little late.
But if you don't mind a word of advice from a lonely
soul, just remember,
Ignorance is bliss.
The woes of the world can't affect you if you don't
know them.

29 The heartbeat of the machine

They are not coming back
It's best for me to move on. But why is it so difficult?
They'll be back in a couple week to drop off more food.
Groan
In my hunger, I drank her nectar. And now she's angry at me. Like I had a choice. It was just too tempting. Its bitterness washed away my sorrow.
Thump
I feel lost.
Look at the sky. Aren't we all? Don't we all just co-exist with the riptide that is life? Going from one job to another, rolling with the punches?
Thump
The waves contorted and ripped.
The TV displayed only static. It said, "It's a weird time to be alive buddy."
I scoffed at him and went outside. "Get a load of that guy. He has no idea what he's talking about." I heard myself mumble as the Moon reached down and kissed my forehead.
Thump

It's alive, like you are.
You think you are alone in your suffering, but so is everyone else.
Why do you not see yourself with the same kindness you see others with?
Thump
And I saw it, fluorescent vapor and highlights, my own night at the opera and I its spectral spectator
Thump
Its gears churn in proud solitude
It sputters oil and steam in refuge
Deeper still I venture and I see
Great pipes and mighty iron curtains
I hear awesome hammering, of Gods and those above my mortal mind
They are melted down and beaten into form, never to lose it.
Molded by the anvil and tempered by the flames.
Thump
They are perfect but capable. Fragile, but resistant.
Thump
Deeper still I venture, through swarms of smoke
Thump
And I find it in throes. Its power was too great for me. I lay my hand on it and whispered to it before it consumes me.
Thump
So that's what that was. I kissed the ground under me.

The waves crash against the rock wall.
One has nothing to do but think.
One has too much to do to think.
Yet we suffer together.

30 Loneliness and madness

We became the gods of this city.
And somewhere along the way,
We forgot how to be human.

Cells.
The neon lights of this landscape haunt me.
All alone, a pillar of dark
In this world of noise.
Each face, blurry yet rigid
The lines of your visage slip away from my fingers
Cells
How can my mind forget you, if my flesh can't?
The world spins and turns,
Seemingly with me
(Absent from it)
The ecstasy of your lips is still fresh on mine
Cells
As I walk this land
Locked forever in dusk
All alone, a pillar of dark
The tall white fountain still plays
In the forgotten world we'd
Built.

As I walk this land,
Plasma filling my veins,
Cells.
Locked
Forever
In
Your lips.
Dark and tall,
The world we'd built.

31 Dart

Down trodden and abandoned.
Left to rot among my own failures.
But I shall move silent, as the night.
Hidden in my mask of lies and deceit
And I shall present, but one dart.
One moment.
One mistake.
One flaw.
And in that moment,
It shall be the blind hands of faith itself.
The hands you trust and have eaten from
That shall strike thee down.
And you shall know
The darkness that surrounded you at your worst has followed you
To your best.
The danger of the path you have chosen,
Oh righteous one,
Beset on all sides by the tyranny of evil men.
Such as I.
And you shall know
It is I,
Death itself.
The marquis of snakes.

Inevitable,
In my everlasting rage.
And you shall know
As I strike in hateful vengeance,
The extent of my wrath
I shall bring you down from glory and you shall bear witness once again to your own failures.
And I shall descend upon thee,
With ravenous hatred.
And in my barbaric cruelty,
I shall find no mercy for those that have wronged me.
And I shall cover each edge of these lands
With your blood.
Until even the infants cries echo with yours and your blood paints the sky crimson.
And then,
I shall leave you in your misery,
For all to see, the fallen one.
And they shall know.
Even Gods bleed.
And they shall remember
The day the devil won.

32 Resonance

This obelisk of glass,
A symbol.
Freedom to some, fear to others.
Neon waterfalls wrap around these fading lands.
Through my shattered window,
I see this land of eternal sorrow,
Molten glass flowing down my face like tears.
Cells.
Galaxies collide as starlight falls like rain,
The universe sings in dissonant tones,
Screaming Moons, bleeding for the sins of man.
Metal, indistinguishable from flesh.
Agonies of architecture, these cold monoliths taunt me
Cells.
And you're running again, the shifting tide of the lost Sun on your back.
The acropolis, of corrupted obsidian and stained marble, looms over your fate.
Threads of light in seas of souls carve a future you cannot see.
Cells.
And perhaps it was destined to be,
Our machinery should never cross,

33 Hazel

Amber and crimson.
Hazel and cherry.
A single note on a lone piano.
Burning at the edge of desire.
Pleasure and happiness flow like rivers here.
The sunlight blankets the sky itself,
Reaching down from its heavenly throne.
A teardrop of ecstasy in the waterfall of creation.
And the wind carries messages long lost.
Stories long forgotten.
Letters never received,
Questions never answered.
Destined to float forlornly,
Scouring for patient ears,
To fall upon.
And as the world turns on its side
To rest once again
The Moon takes the weight of the astral dome on its shoulders,
Shielding these lands from what lies beyond.

34 And behold, a pale horse

Destiny arrives still,
Ever silent on its ebony steed.
And it will move, like a wraith in the night.
And it will strike, as thunder.
A maelstrom of justice.
It shall strike, in its blind fury
Those unfortunate enough to be within its grasp.
And so flows the neon ocean,
This umbral valley of obsidian
Looming over it.
It flows in luminous shades of bliss.
Drowning out the souls of the damned.
It shrieks across this torrid world.
And in its wake, it shall leave the eternal blaze.
Fueled by rancor and love all the same,
It cares not for mortal dwellings.
Each face more contorted than the last,
My eyes are hollow shells,
Unable to see this crystalline world in all its beauty,
In nocturnal light,
I lay awake, staring at my past and future,
Reflected in this lake of desire,
They tread the same path.
How poetic.

35 Solaris and Luna

Twins locked in eternal conflict,
Twisting and turning in serpentine orbits,
Vying for the other's beauty.
They come from a land of no memories,
One where the past and future coil into and past each other,
Doomed to repeat,
Doomed to warp into itself time and time again.
Any hope for change is choked out by the empty world that surrounds them,
The fire of revolution has long since been snuffed.
And the ones that roam this barren land are left scrounging for its embers.
Perhaps a loose spark,
Fighting to reignite the radiant blaze that once led them,
Refusing to accept the eclipse that is upon them.
This valley of shadows and death,
It remembers those that you do not.
Under the shattered sky,
It reaches out, in everlasting agony,
To rid the world of the curse that is its existence.
In this valley where the wind doesn't blow,
Where past and future contort into one,

Where this umbral river flows endlessly,
Where neither the sea nor sky possess stars.
In this land, is a mere spark enough?
Perhaps.
Perhaps it is.

36 Night at the opera

Long has been the journey you have taken.
All through the dark night,
You have pursued this everlasting dream.
To reach what is unreachable.
And even in the web of your dreams,
You weave the same portrait.
To achieve what is unachievable.
But tonight,
Tonight is different.
Were the lights always this bright?
Were your fingers always this limber?
Was the melody always this
Alive?
And suddenly,
As memories overtake your senses,
You catch a glimpse of what you have sought in your solitude.
Your body seems to move on its own.
You close your eyes and find yourself adrift in a sea of radiance.
Each breath is different from the last,
Each note is perfect.
And you feel your heart pumping,
The blood flowing in your veins.

And as the music contours around your body and
takes you with it in its eternal flow,
The lights shine mercy
The air feels alive
Your lungs fill with desire
You can feel each goose bump on your skin
And as the night sky lights up,
The conductor raises his hands
And it is truly
Undeniably
The eternal search is complete;
Perfection.

37 The litany against solitude

Why have you left already?
Is there no joy you find in my company anymore?
Or do you believe this world will be kinder to you
  than I, flaunting what you learned from me?
Come now, let us end this facade.
If it is what you have desired so forlornly,
It is what I shall do.
I will carry this burden for you, too,
Unaided.
For your face gives me the strength I once had,
  and need.

38 Turnstile

Not enough people talk about perspective
Knowing, but feeling powerless even with knowledge.
I know. I know what I should do.
I know my actions hurt only me.
But I was taught to think, not act.

Experience teaches you that
Only after you have reached your goal will you see the beauty in its pursuit, in the journey.

The twinge of forgotten bells echo in my mind
And the temples I built around my memories have long retired into a ceaseless sleep.
This bitter cold and profound vastness I feel,
Is it real?
Is this the very place I set out from?
My skin has forgotten its wind.
My eyes have forgotten its landscape.
How long ago, did I turn my back
On myself?
How long ago, did I empty my hands of emotion?
How long ago, did I rid my shoulders of attachment?
And back again, I find myself.
In the grave of my memories,
I sink into the obsidian sand,

At the beach of regret.
The howling wind paints faces I have long forgotten
Across my eyes.
The bleeding Sun washes a scarlet hue over the sky.
And as the clock strikes midnight,
The tempest shall once again be my friend
And I shall sail across this mighty chasm of lost souls,
Under the guiding light of the unholy eclipse
That shrouds this land,
Locked in dusk,
This land between time
And beyond the stars.
Stuck in an elusive dance with the lady with no visage.
The rotting corpse of God rests here still.
And as once again the Sun rests upon the tortured heads of those who wish to drink its nectar,
Death shall play his hand.
Ambrosia and agony, his twin features,
Atonement for actions across anecdotes
And he will herd his flock
And take the damned to pasture.
On this island
Chained among screaming souls, seething in conjoined solitude, denied sacrament in their foolish sacrilege.
There are none you can trust,
In this twilight world.
Only hope to enslave the sail

And drift away from this purgatory.
And wait until it is the cowl of the abyss
Which drags you back.
Unto this land, locked in dusk.

IV

Scorn

39 Anger

Humiliation. Disgrace
The universe is indifferent to you and your struggle.
There is no god waiting for you.
You cannot change this world of corruption.
Thrash and burn as you might, your insignificance is too great for those above you to even gaze in your direction.
Crimson and obsidian skies, rust and rot grow like a cancer on these decrepit walls, in this derelict kingdom.
The screams of agony scratch and claw at the eroded flash that is the ground.
The permanent eclipse of despair wears down on the twisted shoulders of those that roam this godforsaken land.
The light this world needs to change and heal has long burnt out.
The roaring eye of the Sun watches every speck of dust
In this fallen land of ash and dust.
And on the tenth day in the lake of everlasting embers, I shall arise.
And I shall declare it so,
And it shall be so,
And without mercy,

My iron will shall become divine providence across
the halls of pandemonium
Like blasphemy across God's kingdom,
I will be a thousand bleeding Moons
Against his radiant Sun.

40 Hatred

And light my twisted wings on fire,
As I fall into pandemonium.
And I will show the devil himself
What it means to feel despair and fear.
He will know what it means to be broken and
  ripped apart.
Come demon!
Unsheathe your weapon.
Let us see,
Who is the greater monster.
Let us see,
Who tears the other down first.
Let our battles rip shreds into this plane of reality.
Let us bring down the gates of heaven and hell itself.
And let us not stop.
Not until I am bled dry.
Not until my bones are nothing but specks.
Not until the very air in my lungs has long burnt out.
Not until my heart has long been buried.
Until that very moment,
I will unleash upon this vapid world,
The same unearthly agonies it has dealt unto me.
I will wrench it free from peace and love,
Burn into it, cut my scars of anguish into it,
The marks of justice.

I will show this world what it has created.
Until it is nothing but a desolate husk.
A rotten, scorched wasteland of sin.
Where the fetid rivers of the damned flows free off its edge.
Where the screams of those long forgotten are trapped
Where the fractured Sun brings only disease and scorch to its surface.
Where the twilight Moon only heralds the arrival of the eclipse of humanity.
And everything shall burn and suffer in eternal plight,
With one most of all,
Above them all.
In derelict rule,
Crowned the king of the fallen ones.
Upon his shattered visage, his crown lies
And on countless corpses, his throne.
For he is their salvation, as he is their ruler.

41 Disconnect

This world has lost touch.
It no longer bears any sound or sensation to me,
Not lasting nor fleeting.
And though I speak as you do and laugh as you do,
These words are not mine, and neither is this flesh.
It is but a mask fused into my being,
An amalgamation of atrocities.
And though you can hold out your hand and
meet mine,
And feel the flesh over my bones as it is over yours,
And though this world moves for me as it does
for you,
And though I have all that seems necessary for
being human,
I distinctly lack a soul.
A being.
A heart.
In blinding light and in shrouded night,
In sunrise and dusk,
It is all the same.
And so is my cold emotionless gaze.
This hollow husk of a shell that I occupy,
I only bear it to one day act out my reason.
The truth I have found in all my existence.
I lack what it means to be human.

The voices of that time long gone burn as
I swallow them.
And with my head hung low,
With shame and guilt on my heavy shoulders,
With a deep exhale,
I convince myself.
I am not that person anymore,
Times have changed, and so have I.
I convince myself, I have done nothing wrong.
"I am still a good person."
Yet, when I look in a mirror, I do not recognize what
stares back.
Its dark gaze is not mine,
Its jaunty shoulders are not mine,
Its lanky frame is not mine,
Its thinning hair is not mine,
Its corrupt thoughts are not mine,
Its nervous pacing is not mine,
Its erratic tendencies are not mine,
Its addictions
Not mine
Not mine
Not mine.
But, I know.
Somewhere deep inside me, I know.

Its emaciated face
Is mine.

What have I become?

43 Agony

The idea of making a better world never
appealed to me
It's a constant Karmic cycle,
If you go against the world, the world goes
against you.
Because all study is useless
The Sun will still shine and the birds will still sing
because it's a new day God's Kingdom.
You pray to these false idols like they haven't
abandoned you.
You cling to your faith as if that is what will save you,
redeem your soul.
Let me ask you,
You talk to your "God" so often, how many times has
he talked back?
Tell me,
Will it be your morals that will protect you from the
burning hatred of the lake of fire?
Will it be your love that will save your skin from
being flayed by the whips of fury?
Will it be compassion that tempers your skin until, as
iron, you will learn to love the eternal torment that
awaits you?
Your kind hopes for a better world,
In a universe of unfeeling bitterness.

You continue to search for relief.
I wonder,
How long will it take for your mind to learn
  the truth?

Tell me,
Will it be your prayer that saves you,
In this land where even the priests are deaf
  and blind?

44 Oath

Ochre eyes.
Obsidian skin.
Crystal words and no next of kin.
An idol with an emotion tied to it.
A mere sculpture of beauty.
And a sensation.
One of comfort, of coming home.
And I broke it,
Snapped it in two.
Its shattered visage looks up at me.
They all haunt me.
Imprints in my skin,
Of everyone I've met and done wrong.
Memory is a curse,
One I bear too well.
My regret has never been in my actions, I tell myself.
It is in the world that forced me to make such choices.
The world is a cruel and unjust place and I, simply its agent.
But here I arrive at the crossroads again.
Asking myself if this is me.
I look in mirrors and wonder
"Do I still know you?"
Is it really this world that is wrong?

Is it not my very existence I loathe so dearly?
I am just an agent of my own will.
My mind fragments and drifts further away from reality.
Regret and hatred consume my being as I turn them outwards, to the world.
I will walk this path as many times as I need to.
I swore.

45 Pride

The sin of the Sun.
Who do you think you are?
Standing tall above me?
Whatever fate you have suffered,
I have conquered.
Whatever mountains you have climbed,
I have chiseled from stone.
Whatever oceans you have crossed,
I have braved long before you sough to try.
These hardened eyes of mine,
They hide a tempest behind them.
I see what you really are,
Behind that shameful masquerade of strength and accomplishment.
I see your weakness.
You bear the eyes of one who has not yet seen this world.
Your smile shines with naivety,
And your laugh echoes with ignorance.
Who are you, a mere mortal
To stand before me?
For one should kneel before a king.
This crown that sits on my head,
Would crush you with its weight.
This iron throne,

Would pierce and tear your flesh.
And you can lead an army,
Even in the face of certain death.
But it is I who can lead them to victory.
And when it is your time,
For the eternal sleep,
Then you shall see,
As you look up repent for your sins,
You shall see,
Standing proud in conquest,
The banners of my might.

46 Greed

It was I,
Born to take.
After all,
Why shouldn't I?
This world is mine for the taking,
So that is what I shall do.
Even the land you step on,
The air you breathe,
The possessions you hold so dearly,
It is all meant to be mine.
And I will wait in patient misery,
Watching these heathens trample my treasure.
And I shall strike, when these snakes least expect it.
And my judgment shall be fierce and quick.
I shall take away every drop.
Every grain.
Every speck.
It's all mine.
And inevitably,
It shall return to its rightful ruler.

49 Blizzard

I miss the warmth.
Long and lonely is the odyssey I must complete.
Oh how I long for a time I was unchanged.
Imperfect, but human.
I miss the warmth.
The one on my skin,
The one in my heart and soul.
But I need not suffer.
The question of need has long past,
It is simply one of justice.
Some do not deserve attachment and beauty,
Forsaken forever to see this world in infinite shades of black and grey.
To suffer the bitter cold, the freezing consequence of their own actions.
To only watch what they sacrificed.
To live in perpetual longing and agony.
Hatred my fire and my soul the kindling.
So once again I sit in solitude.
Perhaps this is better for all the denizens of this land.
To rid them of the curse that plagues them.
I can only hope,
They can once again feel the warmth I miss so dearly.

V
Bliss

50 Amber and ambrosia

It is necessary,
Hearing your name.
In whispers and mad rambling.
Necessary to be seen;
In happiness and sorrow alike.
In tears of both joy and sadness.
It is necessary;
To be understood,
Completely and with no filter.
To show someone the parts of ourselves we believe undeserving.
To show someone our scars.
"Show me the valleys in your skin
And I'll show you rivers that'll flow through them."
It is necessary to be vulnerable,
To feel, to cry, to smile and to laugh with no control.
To fight this cold world unalone.
To choose compassion over hatred.
To choose to be kind in a world where one can be anything.
To choose to be better.

51 Of moss and men

I wonder why people do the thing they do?
What compels them?
What makes them act the way they do?
Norms?
Expectations?
Experience?
Isn't free will a myth in this world?
Is it?
Am I really the master of my will?

I do not wish to be, anymore.
I am just lost again.
And if I am lost then my destination matters not.
And if I am adrift then the end matters not.
It is only the journey, the path I take.
The vistas I see and the trails I cross.
The oceans I conquer and the mountains I brave.
Only the steps I have taken.

In midnight auroras and tireless dreams.
In the blazes of shooting stars and the vapor of my
orbit around twilight skies.
And maybe I'd run into you.
And we'd talk and laugh,
And I'd give you my woes and worries.

And you'd fold them into flowers of joy.
Each petal, your love for me.
Don't you worry, I'll cherish it.
Protect it, against the wind and rain.
And one day, I'll give you a flower too.
And there would be no rhyme or reason to it, we'd be together simply because we wanted to.
Plucked from the old rock wall, covered in moss,
Where we grew gardens of love together

52 Midnight dew

If only you knew
The loving envy I feel for you
To laugh so freely
To talk like you do
To live
To be, as you are
To not only see the world's beauty, but to add to it
A knight in shining armor,
You feel like a dream.
A fantasy I made up,
Lying alone with my thoughts and memories.
You feel like everything I wish I was.

To see cruelty and anger and hatred but to choose to be happy regardless,
To choose to be better to be kinder.
It is that I admire.
In your benevolence and patience,
It is you I think of.
In your silence and beauty
It is you I think of,
Unfiltered, unhidden.
It is you I think of

With me.
I don't know, somewhere along the way, you became my comfort.

53 Friends (?)

And we'd talk for days.
And as, with words it began,
With words I'd explore you and you'd explore me.
And it would be a better world,
I'd be honest and we'd both be vulnerable,
In silent joy,
We'd create tapestries of compassion together.
We'd weave parts of ourselves into it,
My scars would blend with yours,
My past would melt into yours,
And we'd be happy together.
Finally understood,
I would realize,
This arduous path that is life,
I cannot save you from it.
I cannot take away your pain,
As much as I wish I could.
The path you have chosen is yours alone to take,
I can only walk along with you.
I cannot be the bonfire,
To chase away sorrow's winter.
But perhaps I can be the lantern,
To spark honesty's warmth in you.

54 Decree

And I hope you realize one day
All that you're capable of.
Everything you deserve,
Gentle snowfall in December,
Warm sunlight in May.
And you'll go far,
These dark nights will just be bad days you
  remember.
Life is a journey, yes
But even journeys can have breaks in them.
After all,
This path is yours to walk
Choose a path that you would love to travel.
This journey is made up of choices.
So make choices worth making.
It'll all just be memories soon.
So make memories worth remembering.
Live a life worth living.
Live free as the stars you wish to join in the night sky.
And let them not forget
That you were here.
That you existed.

I hope you realize one day
All that you can be
And all that you are.
And may you be the guiding light
This lonely tribe needs.

55 So this is love (?)

It feels like coming home, they said.
Like you've been walking your entire life and you can finally rest.
But they lied.
It feels like an alien land,
One of immense beauty and mystery
Every step of the journey,
I find new places of adventure.
The sunlight feels different here,
The people seem kinder.
The sky seem lighter.
Where is it?
This place I find myself?
Like I'm away from my worries
And all my troubles seem insignificant
In contrast to the peace I feel.
And I'll continue on this journey,
Passing great mountains
And while they bear the vestiges of storms,
They stand tall, still.
And though the land was once scorched,
Flowing valleys grow there now.

This place.
This place far away from where I have been all this time.
It makes me feel as though I've been walking my entire life,
And just sat down.

56 Lord of the lies

I don't want to be honest with you.
I don't wish to tell you the truth.
I'd build a castle of deception,
If it meant you would think highly of me
And I would gladly crown myself
The lord of the lies.
I don't wish to shed this armor I have developed over the years.
But its hesitation.
Hesitation I feel.
If it's worth it,
Hiding myself yet again.
I do not wish for you to see
My past, nor my future.
But maybe, we can make the present work together?
Maybe if I stayed right here, in this moment
As the sunlight flows across your face,
Droplets, like gentle whispering.
Maybe if I stayed in your arms a little while longer,
The world would just go away.
The entire room would be filled with light,
How come I never noticed how beautiful you look in amber?
Maybe,
You'd wake up and we would have breakfast together.

We'd be at the table together
And we could be honest.
It's all right. It's just me.
All that strength you have?
You can let it down now.

57 Breathe

Breathe.
You must understand, my friend.
You're alive.
You stand on your own two feet,
See with your own two eyes,
This world does not discriminate against willpower.
Yes, adversity and pain are present,
But so is happiness and joy.
Attachment and love.
There exist ballads on all kinds of pain,
But who sings the song of the joy you feel,
When you see a smile across a face you love?
When you are awoken by a familiar voice speaking in
  your room,
To feel the touch of someone who cares for you as do
  you for them.
To be in the arms of someone who's waiting for you,
To hold the hand of someone who has patiently
  waited to hold yours.
To be with someone
Without deceit,
Without distraction,
Without discretion.
Oh yes,
There are songs on being in love.

Poems on loving someone.
Loving each part of someone as if they're your own.
To trust them with yourself,
As they trust themselves with you.
To breathe as they do,
And to live as they do.

58 Human, once again

I see your face every night.
In unchanging beauty.
In unending distance.
A recreation of memory,
Ripples across your visage.
How I long for what I left behind.
I remember a time,
A lifetime ago,
Back when this unbearable weight did not bear down on me.
Back when I hoped one day to meet you
And together we'd forget.
Leave behind our scars and happiness.
Now just memories.
Memories are all that make up my disheveled form.
How foolhardy is this heart of mine,
Wishing against fate.
Hoping against hope.
Ready, once again, to fight the battles that I have lost.
Even as my mind and body rebel,
Begging for the icy calm of oblivion,
My heart burns on.
Perhaps I am more than I realize.
Oh how it longs,
Not for warmth,

Not for agony, not for hatred.
How it longs to struggle.
To struggle and persist against this cold universe.
How it longs to feel in this unfeeling cosmos.
How easily it forgives me.
How dearly I will protect it.
I will do as I must.
But none will corrupt the one part of me.
The part that is warm.
The part that misses and oh how it longs to once
again be, human.

59 Laid to rest

Locked in this dance with destiny,
The rifts across your face only grow.
But it seems you have reached the end of the line,
traveler.
Perhaps now,
The battle can stop.
Perhaps now,
The crusade you partake in,
Can conclude.
No longer do you need to purge all that you see,
Even if just for a moment.
And it is time now warrior,
Everyone has already left.
Yet you still walk this deserted plain,
Where only your memory keeps you company.
Is this what you wanted?
It is what you have achieved.
So lie now,
Etch these fables into those ancient rock walls.
Let these heroes not be forgotten.
Let their stories not fade with the winds of time,
Into the fleeting land of days past.

So lie still,
In your perfect solitude.
Watch the stars light up the darkness that clouds you so.
May you find that some of their warmth reaches you, too.

Printed at Repro India Ltd.